The Diversity Action Book

The Diversity Action Book

143 THINGS TO GO DO!

A How-To Handbook for Everyone in Your Organization!

JANET CRENSHAW SMITH

FOREWORD BY REV. JESSE L. JACKSON, SR.

A PUBLICATION OF IVY PLANNING GROUP, LLC

Published by
Ivy Planning Group, LLC
15204 Omega Drive, Suite 110
Rockville, Maryland 20850
(301) 963-1669
www.ivygroupllc.com

ISBN 0-9704152-0-6

Printed in the United States of America

Book design by Nita Alvarez

To Gary,
my husband, business partner and best friend

To Gary II, Alex and Bradley,
"the guys"– who keep me centered

To Mama, Daddy and Ronnie,
who taught me early on that I could do anything

In memory of
Dietra and Aunt Ann

FOREWORD

WE STARTED THE WALL STREET PROJECT four years ago to end the multi-billion-dollar trade deficit between leading corporations and minority consumers. Our mission is to expand access to capital to underserved communities that represent market, money, talent, location and growth. We must level and expand the economic playing field for all Americans by increasing minority participation on corporate boards, in executive suites and in the procurement of goods and services.

During the past four years, we have seen that when we replace walls with bridges, everyone wins. Building on our successes, the Wall Street Project has now expanded to include project offices in Washington D.C., Chicago, Atlanta, Cleveland, Los Angeles and San Jose. We have assembled leaders from across the country — representing corporate America, minority business and the community — to work with us to raise key issues and develop strategies for inclusion. This is how I first met Janet and Gary Smith of Ivy Planning Group. Ivy was recruited to participate on the Wall Street Project Steering committee for its strategic planning skills. I recall them as those likely to ask tactical questions like "What will we do and how will we measure our progress?"

That's what THE DIVERSITY ACTION BOOK is all about. We have reached the critical movement — that of economic empowerment. The operative word is movement, i.e., action. Janet Smith describes THE DIVERSITY ACTION BOOK as "not that deep". I disagree. For nearly 40 years, I have been part of a movement in which one or two people have taken small actions, first steps, to knock down huge walls, to open closed doors, to drive enormous change in communities, organizations, cities and nations.

Do not underestimate the power of a single new action. Read THE DIVERSITY ACTION BOOK. Grasp a new idea. Start a movement in your organization, your community, your household and your nation.

REV. JESSE L. JACKSON, SR.

ACKNOWLEDGEMENTS

IN SPRING 1999, the straw finally broke this camel's back. Another innocent voice uttered, "So what do you want me to do?" *To that anonymous voice, I thank you for getting me started. But who knew such a simple book would require so much help to make it to press?*

Everyone at Ivy, like it or not, has lived this process with me. I thank each of you. Jim, Anne, Suki, Reid, Earl, Stephanie, John and Marylinn — thanks for all the emails, post-its and "thinking sessions". Tayna, thanks for binding, scanning, unbinding and rescanning, yet never ever complaining. Leslie and Roxanne, your research capabilities are truly amazing. Much love and thanks, Cynthia and Lorraine, for the late-night brainstorming sessions. Ray and Carolyn, once again, I could count on you for comprehensive explanations and perspectives that countered mine...bless you. And Tom, the occasional nudges really did keep me going.

I am grateful to the many Ivy customers who provided insights and encouragement. Natividad and Ed, thanks for the pushback. Lisa, Jessica and Sunita — great ideas! Neal, thanks for the nudge on indexing the Facilitator's Guide.

Nita, you are beyond patient. Thanks for knowing the answers before I knew the questions. Ah, to be a creative. Thanks to your numerologist as well.

To each contributor — Michele, Ralph, Maggie, Charles, David, Tina, Steve, Oscar, Don, Sheila, Daisy, Kurt, Susan, Farai, Antonio, Tavis — my longtime and new friends, thank you for making this book real for so many people. Congressman Thompson, thank you for your dedication.

To Reverend Jackson — I treasure your mentorship and leadership. On behalf of all of us who have benefited and not thanked you, I do.

Gary II, Alex and Bradley, thanks for understanding, most of the time, why I kept sorting through all those little pieces of paper. Becky, thanks for not throwing them away. And Gary, you define partnership — in business, faith and life — right there cheering me on for yet another "project" that pulled me away and put you in "overload 'cause of Janet" mode, again. You're the best.

INTRODUCTION

THIS BOOK WAS DESIGNED *to respond to the most frequently-asked question in diversity:* "What do you want me to do?"

"Doing Diversity" is not so simple.

I enjoy a challenge. So I launched the diversity practice area in our management consulting firm. I am personally drawn to diversity work because it is the perfect blend of business and people issues. For almost two decades, I have developed business strategies, performance measures, marketing plans and customer-centered realignment processes — the works. Nothing is more complex than diversity implementation. Success in diversity means solving some of today's toughest challenges. My work on this subject has made it clear that organizations need to get down to the basics. To focus on the doing of diversity.

Disagree? If you work for an organization in which even half of the employees are doing even a few of the actions in THE DIVERSITY ACTION BOOK, *consider yourself fortunate. If you care about diversity as a driver of change, as a critical people and business issue of the new millennium, and if you're frustrated because you are not seeing the change happen quickly enough or not at all...then this book was written for you.*

The next time someone says, "I really care about diversity," respond with "What are you doing?" Then, give them a short "To Do" list. Choose just a few from this list of 143 Action Items.

This is a straightforward book filled with simple things you can do to move your organization forward in its diversity journey. The difficulty is not in the complexity of the actions, but taking an action and following it through. It is intended to be easy to read, fun and thought-provoking. You will love some of the actions — you will despise others. In my effort to value others' diversity, I have included some action items that are not even "me". Thank goodness. Actions will touch different readers differently based on their own diversity. This book will reveal your lenses to you.

Use this book in the way that best fits you and your organization. Some of the actions are targeted for an individual; others are team-oriented. We spent months using complex "consultant-like" methodologies to sort the actions. Then I decided that the chaos method was best. (Sorry, Jim and Neal, but the Leader's Guide has an index with Action Items by category.)

Use this book to spark discussion or as a diversity action project for your department. Create a contest or a recognition event around getting some of the actions completed. Close your eyes and randomly select your own Action Item for this month. The "getting started" is more important than the "how you get started". The book is intended to move you off center, to get you to engage — each other, the topic, your commitment to action.

Discussions around diversity have led to many experiences inside and outside the workplace — tears, anger, joy, laughter, eloquent words, not-so-eloquent words, music, "diversity days in the cafeteria", fashion shows — and in some cases, new actions and behaviors that have resulted in meaningful and profitable change.

May this book be a catalyst for you and your organization to add to your "To Do" list of things that actually get done.

JANET CRENSHAW SMITH
Rockville, Maryland

GUEST CONTRIBUTORS

(IN ORDER OF APPEARANCE)

action (ak'shén) n.

1 the doing of something

2 a thing done

3 [pl.] behavior

•

GIVEN THE CHOICE OF

CHANGING

OR

PROVING THAT CHANGE

ISN'T NECESSARY...

MOST PEOPLE

GET BUSY ON THE PROOF.

JOHN KENNETH GALBRAITH

ACTION 1

Dream

A VISION

OF DIVERSITY

SO COMPELLING

EVERYONE WILL

SMILE AND SAY

"WOW"!

MICHELE HUNT
Leadership Change Catalyst and Author of Dream Makers: Putting Vision and Values to Work

ACTION 2

Develop

AN ORGANIZATIONAL

DIVERSITY

VISION, GOALS,

OBJECTIVES

AND MEASURES.

ACTION 3

A TEAM DIVERSITY

VISION

THAT LINKS BACK TO

THE ORGANIZATIONAL

OBJECTIVES.

ACTION 4

THE IMPACT OF DIVERSITY

ON CUSTOMER SERVICE.

Understand how your front-line employees view diversity. Are they respectful of all customers, or do they stereotype – perhaps not treating all customers well? Do front-line employees know that the company values a diverse customer base?

ACTION 5

REDUCE

THE NUMBER

OF PEOPLE WHO SAY,

"SO WHAT DOES DIVERSITY MEAN AT OUR COMPANY?"

This begins with communicating your company's definition of diversity. Will you focus on race and gender? If so, how do you make diversity relevant to the entire workforce? Perhaps you will use a broader definition that includes other dimensions, such as creativity and approach. If so, how do you remain true to those who are traditionally excluded? How do you break the ties?

ACTION 6

Teach

OTHERS ABOUT YOUR DIMENSIONS OF **DIVERSITY.**

ACTION 7

NEW PEOPLE

FOR YOUR

WORK TEAM

AND

PROJECTS.

ACTION *8*

WITH ANOTHER

GENERATION

TO UNDERSTAND

THE SIMILARITIES

AND THE

DIFFERENCES.

ACTION 9

Refuse

TO JOIN IN

THE LAUGHTER

WHEN A JOKE IS

DISRESPECTFUL

OF AN INDIVIDUAL

OR GROUP OF PEOPLE.

ACTION 10

ASK

WHEN YOU'RE

NOT SURE.

IT'S THE BEST WAY

TO GAIN A DIFFERENT

PERSPECTIVE.

ACTION 11

Join

YOUR COMPANY'S

DIVERSITY COUNCIL.

DON'T HAVE ONE? START ONE!

TIPS FOR DIVERSITY COUNCILS:

1. Make sure you have representation from a diverse group of employees – including the lowest levels and the highest; all ages and tenures; and those non-supporters who have not yet bought into the diversity initiative.
2. Establish 6- and 12-month objectives.
3. Achieve a "quick win" within the first six months. Demonstrate that your Diversity Council is a *change agent.*

ACTION 12

Provide

YOUR DIVERSE CANDIDATES

with challenging opportunities.

If your future leaders must first demonstrate an ability to take on challenges, then offer the difficult projects...the risks – **yes, the opportunities to lead** – to a diverse slate of candidates.

PROFESSOR DAVID A. THOMAS
Harvard Business School
Author of
Breaking Through: The Making of Minority Executives in Corporate America

ACTION 13

Document

THE DIVERSITY STRATEGY.

DISTRIBUTE IT.

MAKE IT HAPPEN.

ACTION 14

POST

THREE THINGS

YOUR GROUP

WILL ACCOMPLISH

BY YEAR-END

TO PROVIDE

DIVERSITY

IN YOUR

DEPARTMENT.

ACTION 15

Monitor

the three things

YOU WILL DO

to provide diversity

in your department:

ACTION **DATE**

1 ______________________________ BY __________

2 ______________________________ BY __________

3 ______________________________ BY __________

ACTION 16

STUDY

WHAT OTHER COMPANIES

ARE DOING IN THE

AREA OF DIVERSITY.

BORROW

WHAT APPLIES.

ACTION 17

PAY

FOR PERFORMANCE.

INCLUDE THE

DIVERSITY GOALS,

OBJECTIVES AND MEASURES

IN EVERY MANAGER'S

PERFORMANCE

PLAN.

$$$

HEAR

other perspectives

before

deciding upon

a course of action.

ACTION 19

SURF

THE INTERNET

on an unfamiliar topic you heard about from someone with a perspective different than yours.

ACTION 20

Appoint

WOMEN

to your board of directors –

and make it more than

the quota of

ONE.

catalyst

SHEILA WELLINGTON
President
CATALYST
New York, New York
www.catalystwomen.org

ACTION 21

ASSUME

THE BEST

in people

...even when

they are

very different

from you.

ACTION 22

Know

WHEN TO SPEAK UP.

If there is

NO EVIDENCE

of a commitment

to diversity,

there is

NO COMMITMENT.

ACTION 23

FOR

UNDERSTANDING.

ACTION 24

DECREASE

the number of times

you say, ***"But, it's always***

been done that way."

Sometimes

it sounds

like...

We must hire people from this school!

We could never make money if we targeted THAT MARKET!

A location in THAT NEIGHBORHOOD will never succeed!

ACTION 25

BLEND

TRADITION

WITH

INNOVATION

TO CREATE AN

IMAGINATIVE

ORGANIZATIONAL

CULTURE.

ACTION 26

Attract

NEW CANDIDATES

TO YOUR COMPANY.

Engage *different* "recruiters"

to try *different* approaches

to look for *different* candidates

in *different* places.

ACTION 27

EACH

OTHERS'

DIFFERENCES.

ACTION 28

Remember

the last time

you felt

DIFFERENT –

then make it

EASIER

for the

next person.

ACTION 29

PICK

YOUR HILLS.

BE SELECTIVE.

CHOOSE THE FIGHTS THAT REALLY MATTER,

THE ONES WHERE YOU THINK YOU

CAN BE MOST EFFECTIVE.

DEVELOP DEDICATION AND PASSION

FOR A SPECIFIC ELEMENT OF CHANGE

IN YOUR ORGANIZATION.

TAVIS SMILEY
Host of "BET Tonight with Tavis Smiley", Commentator on "Tom Joyner Morning Show" and Author of
Doing What's Right: How to Fight for What You Believe – and Make a Difference.

ACTION 30

TRAIN

THE ENTIRE WORKFORCE

ON THE DESIRED SKILLS

AND BEHAVIORS.

Get beyond awareness
and focus on outcomes.

Diversity awareness training is good,
but it's not enough.

Make it clear what
you want people to do.

Include practical skills
in your diversity curriculum.

Enhance the training with development
and action learning projects.

ACTION 31

WORSHIP

IN YOUR OWN WAY

AND RESPECT

THE WAYS

OF OTHERS.

ACTION 32

Expect

SUCCESS.

This is not your standard "BE POSITIVE" mantra.

This is the attitude with which
you execute your diversity actions.
When you **expect** to increase market share
by 25%, you won't lower your head
to beg for an inadequate diversity budget.
Instead, you will **confidently** stroll
in with your chest poked out
to request appropriate resources.
When you **expect** different people to
perform well, you won't have that
shocked expression on your face –
"she did *that*?" – when they do.
And, you'll provide fabulous **support**
up-front – the support you now
reserve for the "up-and-coming stars".

ACTION 33

READ

A PUBLICATION

THAT TARGETS A GROUP

THAT IS *NOT* YOURS.

(WE'LL GET YOU STARTED:)

WORKING MOTHER

BLACK ENTERPRISE

OUT

HISPANIC

MINORITIES AND WOMEN IN BUSINESS

METROSOURCE

INDIAN COUNTRY TODAY

JEWISH WEEK

CANEWS

AND HUNDREDS MORE!

ACTION 34

GOODBYE

THE IDEA THAT THINGS WILL RETURN TO THE "GOOD OLD DAYS".

CHANGE IS A REALITY—SO GIVE IT A SMOOCH

AND START TO LOVE IT!

ACTION 35

Differentiate

INDIVIDUALS

FROM

STEREOTYPED

GROUPS.

ACTION 36

SEE

AND ACKNOWLEDGE

HOW YOUR OWN

BIASES

INFLUENCE YOUR

DECISION-MAKING.

ACTION 37

THE FACTS

ABOUT YOUR

EXISTING CUSTOMERS

AND THE

CHANGING

MARKETPLACE.

OUTperform

YOUR COMPETITORS

BY TARGETING

THE FASTEST GROWING

MARKET IN THE U.S.

KURT DEMARS
Publisher
OUT Magazine
New York, New York

ACTION 39

RUN

YOUR MEETINGS A NEW WAY:

- ✔ Invite different people.
- ✔ Let different people "run" it.
- ✔ Insure that different people are "heard".
- ✔ Distribute meeting notes to a more diverse distribution list.

ACTION 40

Stimulate

YOUR MIND

WITH NEW

PERSPECTIVES

FROM

UNLIKELY

SOURCES.

ACTION 41

INSURE

THAT YOUR DIVERSITY STRATEGY

SUCCEEDS BY PROVIDING

THE RESOURCES REQUIRED.

Just as you would push for adequate
resources (people, time, money)
for a new product
(or anything that's good
for your business),
PUSH FOR THIS, TOO.

ACTION 42

FOR

WORK/LIFE

BALANCE.

ACTION 43

PREPARE

YOURSELF

for a surprise

when you

change your

own actions.

OTHERS WILL REACT

DIFFERENTLY TO YOU.

ACTION 44

THE AFFINITY GROUP THAT

BEST SERVES YOUR NEEDS.

VISIT A DIFFERENT

AFFINITY GROUP TO LEARN

SOMETHING YOU DON'T KNOW.

(Affinity groups are formal or informal groups of people who share a common interest, such as a Chinese Culture Club at school or a Gay and Lesbian Group at work.)

ACTION 45

FOCUS

CONVERSATIONS

AND EFFORTS ON

ORGANIZATIONAL

IMPROVEMENTS

FOR THE FUTURE –

NOT ON

MISTAKES

OF THE PAST.

ACTION 46

Trip

STUMBLE AND FALL.

THEN GET UP,

LEARN FROM THE MISTAKE

AND START ALL OVER AGAIN.

IT'S PART OF

DOING BUSINESS

AND IT'S PART OF

THE DIVERSITY JOURNEY.

ACTION 47

WHEN YOUR

DEPARTMENT

IS BENEFITING

FROM DIVERSITY.

WORDS MATTER.

ACTION 48

REWARD

THOSE WHO ARE

MAKING A DIFFERENCE

WITH A

COMPANY

DIVERSITY

RECOGNITION

PROGRAM.

ACTION 49

EXAMINE

your daily interactions

for micro-inequities:

those "little things"

we often do that cause

others to feel devalued.

STEPHEN YOUNG
Director of Diversity
THE CHASE MANHATTAN BANK
New York, New York

ACTION 50

Rotate

JOBS

TO BETTER APPRECIATE THE OTHER PERSON'S CHALLENGES AND POINTS OF VIEW.

ACTION 51

Count

THE DOLLARS YOU SAVE

BY DOING DIVERSITY RIGHT.

QUANTIFY AND DOCUMENT

THE COST SAVINGS AND

NEW REVENUE GENERATION.

102030405060708090100

Receive a spiffy gift when you submit your success story to

www.diversityaction.com

or 1-877-4IVYGRP.

ACTION **52**

Innovate

YOUR PROCEDURES

USING INPUT

FROM

FRONT-LINE

WORKERS AND

CUSTOMERS.

ACTION 53

BEND

BACK YOUR

FINGER WHEN

IT'S POINTING

AT SOMEONE ELSE.

IT'S YOUR

RESPONSIBILITY.

ACTION 54

Watch

WHAT YOU SAY AND DO IN SUPPORT OF DIVERSITY.

Are you using words
that include or exclude?

•

Do your words signal
organizational improvement –
or are they judgmental?

•

Do you honor the value of difference
as you speak about diversity?

ACTION 55

Talk

TO PEOPLE

IN TOTALLY

DIFFERENT PARTS

OF THE ORGANIZATION.

LOOK EVERYWHERE

FOR IDEAS.

ACTION 56

ANNOUNCE

ALL OPPORTUNITIES

that are available

so that **EVERYONE**

has a chance

to succeed.

ACTION 57

MANIPULATE

YOUR NETWORKING

ACTIVITIES SO THAT

YOU MEET PEOPLE

YOU NATURALLY

WOULDN'T.

NEW RELATIONSHIPS

LEAD TO

NEW OPPORTUNITIES.

ACTION 58

Challenge

EVERY DEPARTMENT

TO INCREASE

ITS DIVERSITY

OF NOTEWORTHY

SUPPLIERS.

DON McKNEELY
Publisher
MINORITY BUSINESS NEWS USA
Dallas, Texas

ACTION 59

Mandate

DIVERSITY TRAINING FOR THE CONTRACTORS

WHO DEVELOP YOUR COMPANY MESSAGES, INTERFACE WITH YOUR CUSTOMERS AND MAKE CRITICAL STRATEGIC DECISIONS FOR YOUR COMPANY.

THIS INCLUDES:

AD AGENCIES	TRAVEL AGENCIES
RECRUITING FIRMS	OUTSIDE COUNSEL
PUBLIC RELATIONS FIRMS	EXTERNAL CONSULTANTS

ACTION 60

Consider

DIFFERENT

PERSPECTIVES AND NEEDS

THE NEXT TIME

YOU SELECT

A DATE,

MENU OR TIME

FOR A GROUP FUNCTION.

ACTION 61

Engage

IN CONVERSATION

WITH SOMEONE

YOU DO NOT KNOW

OR WHO IS

DIFFERENT

THAN YOU.

ACTION 62

THE PEACE

WHEN YOU DO NOT AGREE.

DON'T BE AFRAID TO SPEAK UP.

CHANCES ARE, SOMEONE ELSE AGREES WITH YOU.

ACTION 63

SUPPORT

YOUR CO-WORKERS

IN THEIR JOURNEY

ALONG THE DIVERSITY

CONTINUUM.

ALLOW PEOPLE

TO CHANGE

WITHOUT

QUESTIONING

THEIR MOTIVES.

ACTION 64

Lighten

UP!

DIVERSITY INITIATIVES

CAN BE CHALLENGING...

HAVE A LITTLE

FUN WITH THEM

SOMETIMES!

ACTION 65

LET

YOUR DIFFERENCE MAKE A DIFFERENCE.™

INSURING THAT

YOUR DIFFERENCE

HAS AN IMPACT IS

NOT A PASSIVE ACTION.

How will you insure that your

perspective, experience or voice

is reflected in the work you do?

ACTION 66

KEEP

AN OPEN MIND

to the possibility that some of our views
may be out of touch with reality;
that there are better ideas than ours;
and that good ideas come in different
colors, races and genders.

In our increasingly multi-ethnic democracy,
where ideas flourish, true diversity
embraces different ideas, in addition
to people of different colors, races and gender.

SUSAN AU ALLEN
President
U.S. PAN ASIAN AMERICAN
CHAMBER OF COMMERCE
Washington, D.C.

ACTION 67

THE WORKPLACE

BY FOSTERING

HIGH

EXPECTATIONS

FOR

EVERYONE.

ACTION 68

CLICK

ON YOUR

COMPANY'S

DIVERSITY

INTRANET.

ACTION 69

OUT

CONSTRUCTIVE

CRITICISM

FROM

NEW AND DIFFERENT

SOURCES.

ACTION 70

OPEN

YOUR MIND

to new possibilities

and perspectives.

Open the lines of

communication.

TALK!

ACTION 71

PROTECT

YOUR

COMPANY'S

VALUES.

ACTION 72

COMMUNICATE

THE DIVERSITY

VISION, MISSION,

GOALS, OBJECTIVES

AND MEASURES

AT ALL LEVELS

OVER AND OVER

AGAIN.

ACTION 73

Replicate

WHAT'S WORKING

IN OTHER

DEPARTMENTS,

COMPANIES

AND GROUPS.

ACTION 74

Understand

THE QUALITIES

AND COMPETENCIES

OF PEOPLE THAT

TRULY DRIVE

ORGANIZATIONAL

SUCCESS.

BAIL

ON THE

STEREOTYPES.

ACTION 75

Trade

WITH THE

UNDER-UTILIZED

MARKETS RIGHT

UNDER YOUR NOSE.

DIVERSITY MEANS

UTILIZING TALENT

AND BENEFITING

FROM IT.

ACTION 76

RECRUIT

NEW TALENT FROM **NEW** PLACES

TO REALIZE **NEW** BENEFITS.

With the national unemployment rate
running at an astonishingly low 4.1%,
organizations are in need of talent.
But 70% of eligible people with

disabilities are reported **out of work.**
Put 70% beside 4.1%. That's quite a gap.

FIND THE TALENT YOU SEEK IN A NEW PLACE.

CHARLES A. RILEY II, Ph.D
Editor-in-Chief
WE Magazine
New York, New York

ACTION 77

SHARE

YOUR IDEAS

WITH

NEW

PEOPLE.

ACTION 78

Change

THE WAY

YOU

DO

SOMETHING.

ACTION 79

Nominate

YOURSELF

FOR THE

COMPANY

DIVERSITY

AWARD.

ACTION 80

Recognize

YOUR PEERS'

GOOD PERFORMANCE

WITH A

"THANK YOU"

ADVERTISE

in newspapers that reach diverse communities, such as:

The National Newspaper Publishers Association (NNPA)
The Black Press of America
3200 13th Street N.W.
Washington, D.C. 20010
(202) 588-8764
Fax (202) 588-5029
www.nnpa.org

Asian Week
The Voice of Asian America
809 Sacramento Street
San Francisco, California 94108
(415) 397-0220
Fax (415) 395-7258
www.asianweek.com

Indian Country Today
P.O. Box 4250
1920 Lombardy Drive
Rapid City, South Dakota 57703
(888) 550-1311 or (888) 327-1013
www.indiancountry.com

El Diario La Prensa Spanish Daily
345 Hudson, 13th floor
New York, New York 10014
(212) 807-4600
Fax (212) 807-4705

American Jewish Press Association (AJPA)
1828 L Street N.W., Suite 720
Washington, D.C. 20036
(202) 785-2282
Fax (202)-785-2307
www.ajpa.org

India in New York
43 West 24th Street
New York, New York 10010
(212) 741-3742
Fax (212) 627-9503
www.indiainnewyork.com

ACTION 82

PROTECT

THE LAWS

THAT PROTECT

THE DIVERSITY

OF OUR NATION.

HONORABLE
BENNIE G.THOMPSON
U.S. Congress
SECOND DISTRICT OF MISSISSIPPI
www.house.gov/thompson

ACTION 83

LINK

your diversity

strategy

to the

core business

strategy.

ACTION 84

MEASURE

DIVERSITY

WITH THE SAME INSTRUMENTS YOU USE TO MEASURE OTHER BOTTOM-LINE ORGANIZATIONAL INITIATIVES.

ACTION 85

Align

YOUR PERFORMANCE MANAGEMENT SYSTEM WITH THE BEHAVIORS REQUIRED TO ACHIEVE YOUR DIVERSITY *VISION*.

ACTION 86

ISOLATE

those discrete

few things

that you will

ABSOLUTELY

ACCOMPLISH

to make your

vision real.

ACTION 87

Publish

THE ON-GOING

RESULTS OF

YOUR DIVERSITY

INITIATIVE.

LET ALL SHARE

IN THE SUCCESS.

ACTION 88

FIRST THINGS FIRST:

ALLIANCES AND SUPPORT

FOR DIVERSITY INITIATIVES

WITHIN YOUR ORGANIZATION FIRST...

Then, together, you can successfully demonstrate that you are serious about diversifying your relationships in the marketplace. It's hard to demonstrate commitment to diversity on behalf of your corporation if you're standing alone.

OSCAR C. GOMEZ
Vice President,
Office of Diversity
and Business Compliance
Verizon Communications

ACTION 89

SPEAK

UP

WHEN OTHERS

VIOLATE

THE DIVERSITY

GUIDING

PRINCIPLES.

ACTION 90

MIX

YOUR GROUPS.

COMBINE ACROSS

FUNCTIONS, LEVELS

AND DEPARTMENTS TO

BRAINSTORM

YOUR NEXT

DECISION.

ACTION 91

Encourage

NEW IDEAS

BY

REWARDING

CREATIVE

THOUGHT.

ACTION 92

YOUR PARADIGMS

TO TAKE

ADVANTAGE OF

THE *PLETHORA*

OF CHOICES

AND OPPORTUNITIES.

ACTION 93

CHAMPION

THE SUCCESS OF FUTURE LEADERS.

Hispanics will be the largest minority population by 2005. Help our nation's students prepare to face the challenges of the 21st-century work force. The Hispanic Association of Colleges and Universities (HACU) represents more than 240 higher education institutions in the United States, Puerto Rico, Latin America and Spain with high Hispanic enrollment.

Our mission is to promote the development of member colleges and universities; improve access to, and the quality of, post-secondary educational opportunities for Hispanic students; and meet the needs of business, industry and government through the development and sharing of resources, information and expertise.

We are proud to be the "champions" of Hispanic success in higher education.

ANTONIO R. FLORES
President and CEO
HISPANIC ASSOCIATION OF COLLEGES AND UNIVERSITIES (HACU)
San Antonio, Texas
www.hacu.net

ACTION 94

WHISPER

YOUR VIEWPOINT WHEN YELLING ISN'T WORKING.

EFFECTIVE COMMUNICATION HAPPENS WHEN OTHERS *HEAR* YOU.

ACTION 95

DEEPEN

YOUR EXPERIENCES

AND INTERACTIONS

BY ENGAGING IN

OPEN AND HONEST

DIALOGUE.

ACTION 96

Introduce

OTHERS TO

YOUR REALITIES

AND INVITE

THEM TO

SHARE

THEIRS.

ACTION 97

Perfect

THE ART

OF LISTENING

TO

ANOTHER'S

POINT OF VIEW.

ACTION 98

Pamper

YOUR DIVERSITY
CHANGE AGENTS
WITH RECOGNITION,
REWARDS AND
SIMPLE WORDS
OF THANKS.

THEY DESERVE IT.

ACTION 99

SHOUT

YOUR

SUCCESSES

FROM THE

ROOFTOP.

ACTION 100

START

WITH LEARNING.

LEARNING → KNOWLEDGE

KNOWLEDGE → POWER

POWER → GROWTH AND SUCCESS

IT STARTS WITH LEARNING. The success of your business begins and ends with your workforce – the human capital inside your organization. Grow, train and invest in this rich, diverse part of your business and you'll conquer the world!

Set the example for your workforce – make a commitment to learning and celebrate diversity of thought, style and way of life. Join ASTD and our community of learners. Together, we will help your organization increase your knowledge, skills and business performance.

TINA SUNG
President
AMERICAN SOCIETY OF TRAINING AND DEVELOPMENT (ASTD)
1640 King Street, P.O. Box 1443
Alexandria, Virginia 22313
(703) 683-8100 Fax (703) 683-8103
www.astd.org

ACTION 101

MODEL

THE BEHAVIORS

YOU WISH

TO SEE

IN OTHERS.

ACTION 102

ON YOUR

TEAMMATES

WHEN THEY

ACCOMPLISH

THEIR

DIVERSITY GOALS.

ACTION **103**

Celebrate

YOUR HERITAGE

AND THE

UNIQUENESS

OF OTHERS.

ACTION 104

Activate

A SLUGGISH

WORK ENVIRONMENT

WITH AN

INNOVATIVE

SOLUTION:

THE ONE OTHERS SAY

"WILL NEVER

WORK HERE."

ACTION 105

THINK

about

new ways

to use

the resources

at your

disposal.

ACTION 106

TUNE-UP

YOUR CONFERENCES AND MEETINGS WITH DIVERSE SPEAKERS, TOPICS, MUSIC AND FOOD.

MAGGIE MUZIKOWSKI
Director of EEO/Diversity
Pennzoil-Quaker State
Houston, Texas

PENNZOIL-QUAKER STATE
COMPANY

ACTION *107*

Initiate

A CHANGE

IN YOUR ORGANIZATION

THAT WILL

BENEFIT

SOMEONE

OTHER THAN YOU.

ACTION 108

RAISE

YOUR EXPECTATIONS

AND STANDARDS

FOR THOSE

WHO ARE DIFFERENT.

STOP BEING SO

"PLEASANTLY

SURPRISED."

ACTION 109

Review

COMPANY POLICIES

TO INSURE

THEY *ALIGN*

WITH YOUR

DESIRED DIVERSITY

OUTCOMES.

ACTION 110

Look

for **NEW** markets

in **NEW** places

for **NEW**

possibilities

and profits.

ACTION 111

TO MAKE THE SAME

OLD MISTAKES.

MAKE NEW ONES.

CREATIVITY AND INNOVATION,

I.E., DIVERSITY OF THOUGHT,

FLOURISH WHEN PEOPLE ARE ALLOWED –

IN FACT, ARE ENCOURAGED –

TO TAKE A "CHANCE".

ACTION 112

Traverse

A NEW PATH

while valuing the trails

blazed by those

who came before you.

ACTION 113

YOUR OWN HORN

when you've

accomplished

one of your

diversity

action items.

ACTION 114

THE DIVERSITY

JOURNEY!

THE BENEFITS

FAR OUTWEIGH

THE CHALLENGES.

IT'S A PLEASURE.

ACTION 115

CLOSE

OFF ALL ROADS

THAT LEAD

TO

DISRESPECT

AND HATRED.

ACTION 116

Value

DIFFERENCE

AS A

COMPETITIVE

ADVANTAGE.

ACTION 117

Appreciate

THE BEAUTY OF A WORLD

THAT OFFERS SUCH

A WIDE SPECTRUM

OF PERSPECTIVES

AND THE

OPPORTUNITIES

THEY BRING.

BE

MINDFUL

OF YOUR

INDIVIDUAL IMPACT.

YOUR POWER

TO MAKE

CHANGE HAPPEN.

ACTION 119

NOT STOP

WHEN YOU LEARN

YOUR HISTORY.

ALL OUR HISTORIES

ARE INTER-RELATED AND

KNOWLEDGE WILL SET US FREE.

FARAI CHIDEYA
Author of
The Color of Our Future

ACTION *120*

YOURSELF

IN DIFFERENCE

TO STRENGTHEN

YOUR OWN WEAKNESSES.

WRAP YOURSELF

IN DIVERSITY

TO CREATE A SYNERGY

OF STRENGTHS.

ACTION 121

BOUNCE

BACK

WHEN THINGS

DON'T WORK.

SOMETIMES

THE ROAD WON'T BE CLEAR

FOR YOUR

DIVERSITY JOURNEY.

ACTION 122

$AVE

TIME AND MONEY

BY INCORPORATING

DIFFERENT VIEWS

INTO DECISIONS.

Fret NOT.

Diversity

can be difficult

to understand

and put into practice.

ACTION 124

Learn

FROM PAST

INJUSTICES

AND FOCUS ON

TODAY'S POSSIBILITIES.

Visit The Holocaust Museum.

Read Black Labor, White Wealth

by Dr. Claud Anderson.

ACTION 125

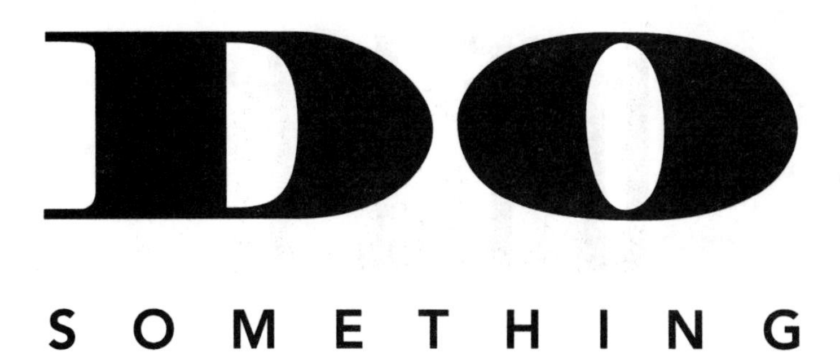

SOMETHING

TO

IMPROVE

YOUR WORK

ENVIRONMENT.

ACTION 126

HELP

OTHERS

BECOME AWARE

OF THEIR

BLIND SPOTS.

ACTION 127

VOLUNTEER

YOUR TIME

AND EXPERTISE

TO OTHERS.

RALPH DICKERSON
President
UNITED WAY OF NEW YORK CITY
New York, New York

ACTION 128

Realize

THAT VALUING

DIVERSITY

BENEFITS

EVERYONE.

NO ONE IS LEFT OUT.

ACTION 129

Reveal

YOUR

UNIQUENESS

SO OTHERS

CAN APPRECIATE IT.

ACTION 130

Acknowledge

YOUR FAULTS.

MAKE IT OKAY

TO BE "WRONG"

IN YOUR ORGANIZATION.

IT WILL MAKE FOR A MORE

CREATIVE AND

INNOVATIVE

CULTURE.

ACTION 131

BLOCK

THOSE WHO WANT TO MAINTAIN THE STATUS QUO – CONTINUE TO STRIVE FOR GROWTH AND EXCELLENCE.

ACTION 132

Translate

FOR SOMEONE WHEN THEY

DON'T GET IT,

AND YOU DO.

(but be careful when you think

you're the only one

who gets it.)

ACTION 133

Bite

your tongue

once in

a while.

ACTION 134

Adjust

YOUR PROGRAMS

FOR

DYNAMIC

TIMES.

BE FLEXIBLE.

ACTION 135

Walk

THE TALK.

YOU'LL

TRAVEL *FARTHER*

THAN YOU

THINK.

ACTION 136

Hold

YOUR MANAGERS ACCOUNTABLE

for building an inclusive culture that leverages the diversity of your people. INSURE that leaders identify, develop and utilize diverse employee talent as part of a winning, high-performing team strategy.

DAISY M. JENKINS
Director of Global Diversity
RAYTHEON
Lexington, Massachusetts

ACTION 137

ANTICIPATE

OBJECTIONS

FROM UNLIKELY

SOURCES.

EVEN THOSE WHO

MIGHT BENEFIT

SOMETIMES

OPPOSE CHANGE.

ACTION 138

TO

INTOLERANCE

IN A

RESPECTFUL

WAY.

GRADUATE

from diversity "PROGRAMS"

to a full-fledged

DIVERSITY INITIATIVE

with strategy,

process and

policy alignment,

measurement

and accountability.

CHECK

WWW.DIVERSITYACTION.COM

FOR

UP-TO-DATE

INFORMATION

ON

BEST PRACTICES

IN DIVERSITY.

ACTION 141

Decorate

YOUR OFFICE WITH

DIVERSITY ACTION

POSTERS.

(143 TO CHOOSE FROM!)

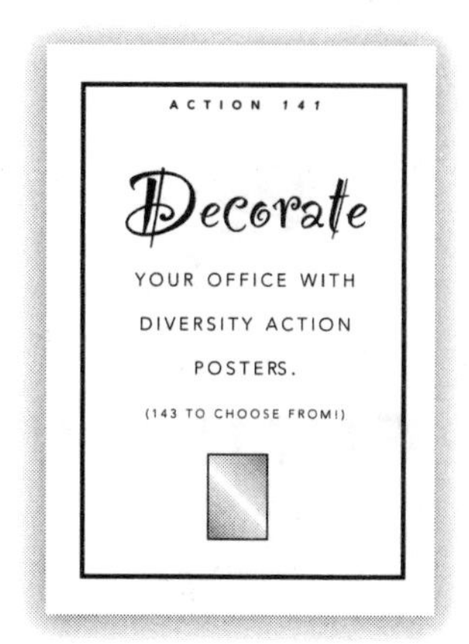

ACTION 142

INCREASE

YOUR CHANCES

TO BE RIGHT –

OR WRONG:

DO SOMETHING!

ACTION 143

GET

B U S Y

AND SELECT A

DIVERSITY ACTION

NOW!

The Diversity Action Book

FACILITATOR AND LEADER'S GUIDE

Designed for Non-Diversity Practitioners

✔ Managers ✔ Team Leaders ✔ Change Agents

✔ Facilitators ✔ Diversity Councils

Completely self-contained

Requires no prerequisites

Provides a Roadmap for Discussion of

THE DIVERSITY ACTION BOOK

✔ Index of the 143 Action items for easy reference

✔ Considerations and further explanations of each Action

✔ Suggested Questions ✔ Activities and Exercises

The Diversity Action Book

ORDER FORM

QUANTITY	COST
1 to 99 books	$14.95 each
100 to 999	$13.95 each
1,000 or more	$12.95 each

No. of Books ____________

Total Amount $____________

S/H Charges* $____________
(see chart at right)

TOTAL DUE $____________

Maryland residents add 5% sales tax $____________

Maryland TOTAL $____________

All orders shipped via UPS Ground. For Next Day and Second Business Day delivery or delivery outside the continental U.S., please call (877) 448-9477.

FOUR WAYS TO ORDER:

Call Toll-free: **(877) 448-9477**

Fax: **(301) 963-8068**

Online: **www.diversityaction.com**

Mail Check/Money Order payable to:

IVY PLANNING GROUP
15204 Omega Drive, Suite 110
Rockville, Maryland 20850

SHIPPING AND HANDLING
***(S/H CHARGES)**

Order Amount	S/H Charge
Up to $50	$ 5
$50 - $99	8
$100 - $249	12
$250 - $749	18
$750-$1,299	32
$1,300 - $1,999	55
$2,000 - $3,499	68
over $3,500	Call

Please send more information on other products and services to help turn Diversity into Action:

- ☐ *Diversity Action Book Facilitator and Leader's Guide*
- ☐ *Diversity Action Workshops and Classes*

PLEASE PRINT CLEARLY

NAME ____

ADDRESS ____

CITY ____________________ STATE ____________ ZIP ____________

PHONE (   ) ____________________ FAX (   ) ____________________

EMAIL ____

☐ MasterCard ☐ VISA ☐ American Express ☐ Check/Money Order enclosed

Acct. No. ________ - ________ - ________ - ________ Expiration Date ____________

Signature X ____

Prices effective September 2000 and are subject to change. Orders payable in US dollars.